6

LET'S GO

Workbook

Steve Wilkinson

Karen Frazier

Barbara Hoskins

Ritsuko Nakata

OXFORD
UNIVERSITY PRESS

SECOND EDITION

M000187487

Let's Talk

A. Fill in the blanks.

You can use some words more than once.

took	was	liked	can't	did	Did

Hello, Mike.
When _____ you get back?

Yesterday evening.

How _____ Australia?

It _____ great.
I _____ a lot of pictures.

I _____ wait to see them.

_____ you get my postcard?

Yes, I _____.
I _____ the stamp a lot.

B. Change the words.

1. walk → <u>has walked</u>

2. wash → _____

3. feed → _____

4. eat → _____

5. clean → _____

6. be → _____

7. see → _____

8. finish → _____

9. take → _____

10. go → _____

C. Make sentences.

Use "already" and "yet."

1. take a bath

   He hasn't taken a bath yet.

   She has already taken a bath.

2. feed the dog

   _____

   _____

3. eat dinner

   _____

   _____

4. go shopping

   _____

   _____

D. Write the questions and answers.

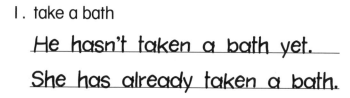

1. _Has she washed her hands_

   yet? No, she hasn't.

2. _____

   _____

3. _____

   _____

4. _____

   _____

A. Make two lists.

October three years five months 1991 Wednesday two o'clock six days an hour

since

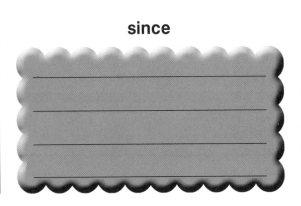

for

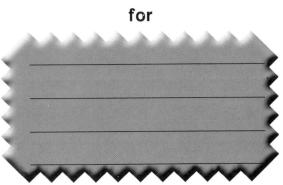

B. Complete the sentences.
Use "for" or "since."

 1. Mary has had a cat

_____ two weeks.

 2. Martin has had a cold

_____ three days.

 3. Evan has had a pen pal

_____ September.

 4. Norma has collected stamps

_____ three years.

 5. Bob's father has been a

doctor _____

1985.

 6. Brian has been on the train

_____ five

o'clock.

 7. Jenny has been in sixth

grade _____

one month.

 8. Anna has been at math

camp _____

Saturday.

C. What about you?
Think of a question and write the answer.

How long have you _____?

_____

D. Answer the questions.

Use "for" or "since."

1. How long has Peter been on the soccer team?

   He has _____ two months.

2. How long has Lee lived in Taiwan?

   _____ 1992.

3. How long has Sara studied Spanish?

   _____ May.

E. Make sentences.

Write sentences with the same meaning. Use "for" or "since."

1. Today is Wednesday. Jack has had a cold
   since Monday. *Jack has had a*
   cold for three days.

2. Now it's 1999. Linda has been a teacher
   for five years. _____

   _____

3. Now it's May. Mark has lived in London
   for three months. _____

   _____

4. Now it's 7:40. Sue has been on the phone
   since 6:40. _____

   _____

A. Fill in the blanks.

Jason is asking Pete about his hobby for the *Newburg News*.

Use the information below to complete the article.

Jason: What is your hobby, Pete?

Pete: Skiing.

Jason: How long have you gone skiing?

Pete: For four years. I go skiing every winter.

Jason: Why do you like skiing?

Pete: It's very exciting. I especially like the mountains.

Jason: Who do you go skiing with?

Pete: I go with my family. And I like meeting new people on skiing trips. Sometimes they are experienced skiers. Sometimes they are beginners.

The Newburg News

Pete Brown's _____

Pete Brown's _____ is skiing. He has gone skiing every

_____ for _____ _____. Pete likes skiing

because it is very _____. He _____ likes the

mountains.

He goes skiing with _____ _____. He also likes

meeting _____ _____. Sometimes they are _____

skiers. Sometimes they are _____ and it is their first

time on a skiing trip.

Unit I

B. Check "True" or "False."
Use the information on page 6.

1. Pete has gone skiing for four years.	☐ True	☐ False
2. Pete goes skiing with his family.	☐ True	☐ False
3. Pete goes skiing every spring.	☐ True	☐ False
4. Pete doesn't like the mountains.	☐ True	☐ False
5. Beginners can go on skiing trips.	☐ True	☐ False
6. Pete doesn't like meeting new people.	☐ True	☐ False

C. What about you?

1. Have you ever been skiing?

_____

2. Do you like meeting new people?

_____

D. Circle and write.

1.    th   tch   _____

2.    th   tch   _____

3.    th   tch   _____

4.    th   tch   _____

5. 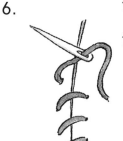   th   tch   _____

6. 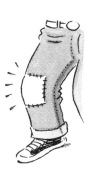   th   tch   _____

Fill in the blanks.

For each picture, use four words with the same ending sound.

two	Italy	a bakery	1995
four	Sunset Drive	a candy store	1992
three	Honolulu	a beehive	1984
five	Singapore	the city zoo	1983

1. She's known him since she was <u>two</u>.

   She met him in <u>Honolulu</u>.

   They got married in <u>the city zoo</u>.

   They had a baby in <u>1992</u>.

2. She's known him since she was _____.

   She met him in _____.

   They got married in _____.

   They had a baby in _____.

3. He's known her since he was _____.

   He met her in _____.

   They got married in _____.

   They had a baby in _____.

4. He's known her since he was _____.

   He met her in _____.

   They got married in _____.

   They had a baby in _____.

Unit 1

A. Make sentences.

Use "already" or "yet."

1. eat dinner

He _____

2. finish his homework

He _____

3. wash the dishes

She _____

4. feed the dog

She _____

B. Circle and write.

 1. Peter has collected coins since he was seven years old. Now he is eleven. How long has he collected coins?

a) four years   b) six years   c) seven years

He has _____

_____

 2. Liza has been at summer camp since Saturday. Today is Thursday. How long has Liza been at camp?

a) three days   b) six days   c) seven years

_____

_____

 3. Ray has studied piano for six months. He started in April. What month is it now?

a) April   b) June   c) September

_____

_____

 4. Ellen has had a dog since she was eight years old. She has had the dog for three years. How old is she now?

a) eight   b) three   c) eleven

_____

_____

Let's Talk

A. Fill in the blanks.

You can use some words in the box more than once.

tastes	sounds	feels	smells	looks

1.

It _____ beautiful.

2.

It _____ wonderful.

3.

It _____ awful.

4.

It _____ sour.

5.

It _____ soft.

6.

It _____ sweet.

B. Fill in the blanks.

1.

sound	sounds	hear

Liz: What do you _____?

Ted: I _____ music.

Liz: How does it _____?

Ted: It _____ wonderful.

2.

looks	see	look

Liz: What do you _____?

Ted: I _____ a rainbow.

Liz: How does it _____?

Ted: It _____ beautiful.

3.

smells	smell

Liz: What do you _____?

Ted: I _____ garbage.

Liz: How does it _____?

Ted: It _____ awful!

C. Fill in the blanks. Complete the crossword.

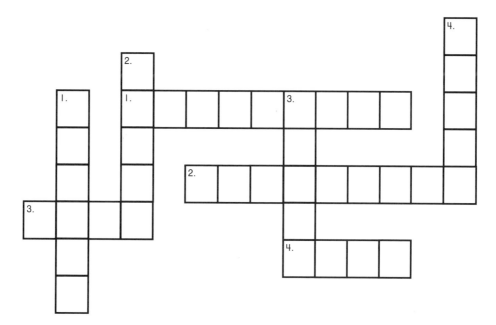

Across

1. How does the music sound?

   It sounds _____.

2. How does the lake look?

   It looks _____.

3. How does the blanket feel?

   It feels _____.

4. How does the rock feel?

   It feels _____.

Down

1. How does the paper feel?

   It feels _____.

2. How does the ice cream taste?

   It tastes _____.

3. How does the bark feel?

   It feels _____.

4. How does the garbage smell?

   It smells _____.

Let's Learn

A. Fill in the blanks.

1. fast	faster	the fastest
2. tall	_____	_____
3. colorful	_____	the most colorful
4. _____	more delicious	the most delicious
5. _____	better	_____
6. beautiful	_____	_____
7. _____	_____	the worst
8. interesting	_____	_____

B. Write the names.

Read the sentences. Then label each T-shirt with the right name.

Mike's T-shirt is colorful.

Brian's T-shirt is more colorful than Mike's.

Pete's T-shirt is the most colorful.

1. _____'s T-shirt   2. _____'s T-shirt   3. _____'s T-shirt

C. Make sentences.

Jane's cake   Selma's cake   Beth's cake

1. Beth's cake is delicious _____.

2. _____

3. _____

D. Draw and answer.

Draw three flowers.

Which one is the most beautiful? Circle the most beautiful flower.

Draw three pictures.

Which one is the most interesting? Circle the most interesting picture.

E. Answer the questions.

Richard's flowers   Penny's flowers   Kathy's flowers

1. Which flowers look the best?

_____

2. Which flowers look the worst?

_____

A. Find and circle the words.

| skills |
| visually-impaired |
| disabilities |
| trainer |
| obstacle |
| hearing-impaired |
| cross |

a	m	o	r	r	m	o	z	a	m	u	y	t	q	w	e	t
c	a	b	d	a	n	g	a	r	p	r	t	a	t	u	e	r
v	i	s	u	a	l	l	y	i	m	p	a	i	r	e	d	a
y	q	t	e	l	o	u	a	n	i	x	y	s	a	r	u	i
p	r	a	l	n	s	v	e	g	l	b	s	k	i	l	l	s
i	f	c	r	o	s	s	t	i	t	e	r	e	n	a	v	t
k	g	l	y	z	d	i	s	m	f	i	l	l	e	s	r	o
a	h	e	e	l	o	f	i	p	l	m	k	c	r	a	c	l
y	h	e	a	r	i	n	g	i	m	p	a	i	r	e	d	o
u	u	z	d	i	s	a	b	i	l	i	t	i	e	s	h	c

B. Unscramble the words.

1. n e i h r a g   g d o = _____

2. i e g d u   o d g = _____

3. a n t i r n g i   c h s o l o = _____

C. Fill in the blanks.
Use the words above.

Mr. Clark is a dog _____. He has a _____ _____ for dogs.

His dogs are named Bruno and Nikki. They are learning _____ to help people with

_____. Bruno is a _____ _____. He is learning to help

_____ people. He can help a person _____ a busy street or walk around an

_____. Nikki is a _____ _____. She can tell a _____

person when the telephone rings or when someone knocks on the door.

D. Write the questions or answers.

1. <u>Who</u> _____

    He is a dog trainer.

2. Where does a guide dog learn its skills?

    _____

3. _____

    No, she isn't. Nikki is a hearing dog.

4. Do guide dogs help hearing-impaired

    people? _____

E. Check the correct boxes.

	Hearing Dog	Guide Dog
1. This dog helps hearing-impaired people.	☐	☐
2. This dog helps visually-impaired people.	☐	☐
3. This dog helps people cross a busy street.	☐	☐
4. This dog tells people when the telephone rings.	☐	☐
5. This dog tells people when someone knocks on the door.	☐	☐
6. This dog helps people walk around an obstacle.	☐	☐

F. Unscramble, match, and write.

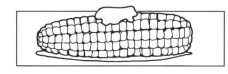   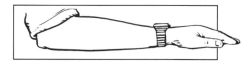

_____   _____

_____   _____

   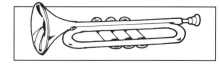

_____   _____

Let's Chant

Use the code to fill in the blanks.

Code																									
a	b	c	d	e	f	g	h	i	j	k	l	m	n	o	p	q	r	s	t	u	v	w	x	y	z
↓	↓	↓	↓	↓	↓	↓	↓	↓	↓	↓	↓	↓	↓	↓	↓	↓	↓	↓	↓	↓	↓	↓	↓	↓	↓
e	f	g	h	i	j	k	l	m	n	o	p	q	r	s	t	u	v	w	x	y	z	a	b	c	d

1. This one's _____, but that one's _____.
   c k k z   x a p p a n

2. This one's _____, but that one's _____.
   x w z   s k n o a

3. This one's _____, but that one's
   e j p a n a o p e j c

   _____.
   i k n a   e j p a n a o p e j c

4. This one's _____
   p d a   i k o p   x a w q p e b q h

   _____.
   k b   w h h

5. This one's _____, but that one's
   z a h e y e k q o

   _____.
   i k n a   z a h e y e k q o

6. This one's _____.
   p d a   x a o p   k b   w h h

Let's Listen

A. Complete the questions.

Read the answers. For each question, use one word from each box.

~~looks~~	~~feels~~
~~smells~~	~~tastes~~

~~hard~~	~~awful~~
~~beautiful~~	~~sweet~~

1. Which one __Smells__ __awful__ , a (skunk) or a flower?
   A skunk.

2. Which one __tastes__ __sweet__ , a grapefruit or (ice cream?)
   Ice cream.

3. Which one __feels__ __hard__ , a blanket or (a rock?)
   A rock.

4. Which one __looks__ __beautiful__ garbage or (a rainbow?)
   A rainbow.

B. Read the sentences. Fill in the prize numbers.

1.

Sue's cake

Tom's cake

Kay's cake

Kay's cake was good, but Sue's cake was better. Tom's cake was the best of all.

2.

Ted's painting

Erica's painting

Ken's painting

Ken's painting was more beautiful than Ted's painting. Erica's painting was
the most beautiful of all.

Let's Review

A. Write the answers and complete the maze.

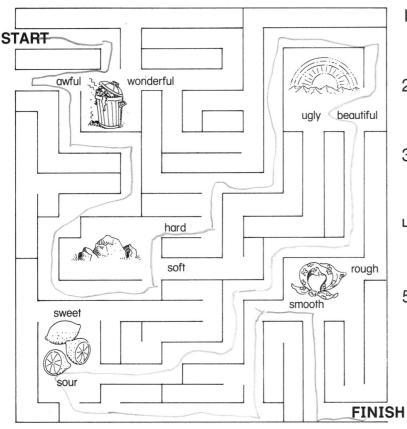

START

awful   wonderful

ugly   beautiful

hard

soft

rough

smooth

sweet

sour

FINISH

1. Does trash smell wonderful or awful?

   awful

2. Does a rock feel hard or soft?

   hard

3. Does a rainbow look beautiful or ugly?

   beautiful

4. Does a lemon taste sweet or sour?

   sour

5. Does silk feel rough or smooth?

   smooth

B. Complete the questions. Write the answers.

1. How does it ___feel___?

   It feels soft.

2. How does it _Sound_?

   beautiful

3. How does it _look_?

   beautiful

4. How does it _smell_?

   beautiful

5. How does it _feel_?

   rough

6. How does it _taste_?

   perfect

C. Read the sentences and fill in the blanks.

4 years old	moved to Tokyo
5 years old	got a pet dog
6 years old	started piano lessons
7 years old	learned how to _____
8 years old	started to _Collected coinse_
9 years old	started English lessons
10 years old	joined the soccer team
11 years old	started to _____

This is Kenji. He is 12 years old now. Kenji has collected coins since he was eight. He has ridden a bicycle for five years. He has played computer games since he was eleven years old.

D. Answer the questions.
Look at the information above. Use "since."

1. How long has Kenji studied piano?

   He has _____ since he was _____

2. How long has Kenji lived in Tokyo?

   _____

3. How long has Kenji had a dog?

   _____

4. How long has Kenji been on the soccer team?

   _____

E. Fill in the blanks. Use "for."

1. Kenji has had a dog _for seven years._ _____

2. Kenji has lived in Tokyo _____

3. Kenji has collected coins _____

4. Kenji has studied English _____

Let's Talk

A. Match and connect.

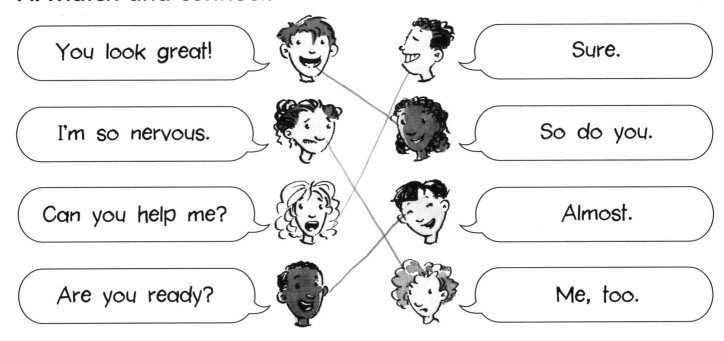

You look great!		Sure.
I'm so nervous.		So do you.
Can you help me?		Almost.
Are you ready?		Me, too.

B. Fill in the blanks.

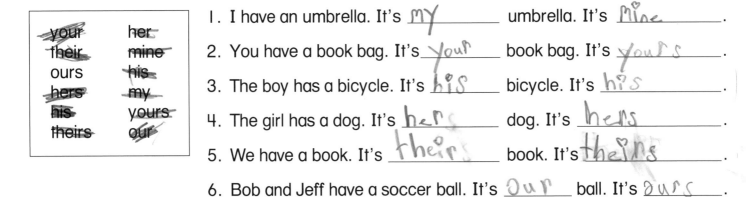

your	her
their	mine
ours	his
hers	my
his	yours
theirs	our

1. I have an umbrella. It's _my_ umbrella. It's _Mine_.
2. You have a book bag. It's _your_ book bag. It's _yours_.
3. The boy has a bicycle. It's _his_ bicycle. It's _his_.
4. The girl has a dog. It's _hers_ dog. It's _hers_.
5. We have a book. It's _theirs_ book. It's _theirs_.
6. Bob and Jeff have a soccer ball. It's _our_ ball. It's _ours_.

C. Connect and write.

1. Whose boots are these?

   _____

2. Whose house is this?

   _____

3. Whose cap is this?

   _____

D. Find and circle the words. Label the pictures.

vest	apron
sombrero	shawl
gloves	belt

s	h	a	w	l	i	g	l	o	v	e	s
b	c	e	x	s	o	m	b	r	e	r	o
e	s	u	n	q	a	l	s	e	s	i	o
l	a	p	r	o	n	b	e	l	t	q	p

1. _____

2. _____

3. _____

4. _____

5. _____

6. _____

E. Make sentences. Match and connect.

Wendy

Mike

Ray

Julia

Jim and Dorothy

1. It's Ray's belt.

   It's his belt. _____   It's his. _____

2. It's Wendy's scarf.

   _____   _____

3. They're Julia's sandals.

   _____   _____

4. It's Jim and Dorothy's umbrella.

   _____   _____

5. They're Mike's cowboy boots.

   _____   _____

Let's Learn

A. Fill in the blanks.

1. Mexico → <u>Mexican</u>   2. Africa → _____   3. Korea → _____

4. India → _____   5. China → _____   6. Japan → _____

B. Make sentences. Use one word from each box.

sing	eat	play
tell	do	play

Chinese	African	Mexican
Japanese	Indian	Korean

instrument	game	curry
dance	story	song

1. <u>She is doing a Japanese</u>
   <u>dance.</u>

2. _____

   _____

3. _____

   _____

4. _____

   _____

5. _____

   _____

6. _____

   _____

C. Fill in the blanks.

1. Which woman is Nathan's mother?

   She is the woman who is doing a Japanese dance.

   Her name is _____

2. Which man is Nathan's father?

   He is the man who is telling a Korean story.

   _____

3. Which woman is Nathan's aunt?

   She _____

   Her name is Sara.

4. Which boy is Nathan's older brother?

   _____

   His name is Brian.

5. Which man is Nathan's uncle?

   _____

   His name is Steve.

Let's Read

A. Look at the code. Write the words.

Code																									
a	b	c	d	e	f	g	h	i	j	k	l	m	n	o	p	q	r	s	t	u	v	w	x	y	z
↓	↓	↓	↓	↓	↓	↓	↓	↓	↓	↓	↓	↓	↓	↓	↓	↓	↓	↓	↓	↓	↓	↓	↓	↓	↓
z	a	b	c	d	e	f	g	h	i	j	k	l	m	n	o	p	q	r	s	t	u	v	w	x	y

Example: d b u = cat

1. q s j o d j q b m = _principal_

2. t f s w f e = _____

3. g f t u j w b m = _____

4. u b d p t = _____

5. g b t i j p o = _____

6. o p p e m f t = _____

7. j o u f s o b u j p o b m = _____

8. q f s g p s n f e = _____

B. Fill in the blanks.

Use the words above to complete the story.

You can use some words more than once.

Newburg School had its annual _____ _____ last Saturday. Students _____ food from many different countries. They _____ curry, _____, sushi, _____, and many other _____ foods. Several student groups _____. There was African dancing, Japanese storytelling, and a Javanese puppet show. There was also an _____ _____ show. Students modeled clothing from many different countries. Everyone had a great time. Mr. Jones, the school _____, said, "All of our students did a wonderful job."

C. Write the questions or answers.

1. When did Newburg School have its annual international festival?

   _____

2. _____

   They served curry, tacos, sushi, noodles, and other international foods.

3. Who modeled clothing?

   _____

4. _____

   He is the school principal.

5. What did Mr. Jones say?

   _____

D. Circle.
Which word is different? Circle one word in each line.

1. | curry | sushi | puppets | noodles |

2. | dancing | performed | singing | storytelling |

3. | noodles | African | Javanese | Japanese |

4. | tacos | sombrero | vest | scarf |

E. Unscramble the words and fill in the blanks.

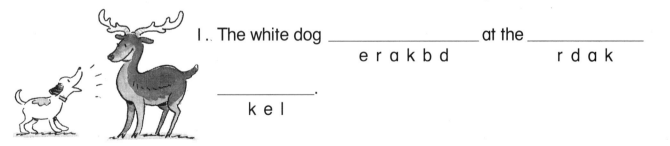

1. The white dog _____ at the _____
   e r a k b d   r d a k

   _____ .
   k e l

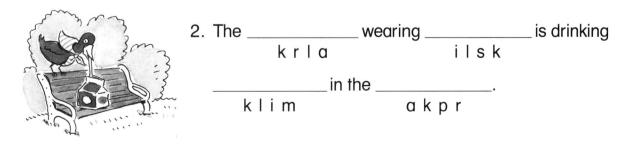

2. The _____ wearing _____ is drinking
   k r l a   i l s k

   _____ in the _____ .
   k l i m   a k p r

Let's Sing

A. Fill in the blanks.

You can use some words more than once.

| whose | my | mine | your | yours |

Whose cowboy boots are these?

They're _____.
They're my boots.

_____ hat is this?

It's mine.
It's _____ hat.

Are these _____ gloves?

No, they're not. They're not _____. They're _____.
They're your gloves.

Is this _____ shawl?

Yes, it is. It's yours.
It's _____ shawl.

B. Match and connect.

Connect the clothes to the girls. Use the information above.

Let's Listen

A. Match and connect.

1. It's my vest. •   • They're mine.

2. They're her boots. •   • It's mine.

3. They're my sandals. •   • It's hers.

4. It's her umbrella. •   • It's his.

5. It's his belt. •   • They're hers.

B. Answer the questions.

1.  Whose scarf is this?

   It's hers.

2. Whose boots are these?

   _____

3.  Whose sombrero is this?

   _____

4.  Whose sandals are these?

   _____

C. Complete the sentences.

Richard   John

Paul

George

1. John is the boy who is playing the guitar.

2. Paul _____

   _____

3. Richard _____

   _____

4. George _____

   _____

Let's Talk

A. Answer the questions.

water the garden
pick apples
feed the pigs
go swimming
eat lunch
brush the horses
milk the cows
gather the eggs

1. What did Joe do before he gathered the eggs?

   He milked the cows before he gathered the eggs.

2. What did Joe do after he fed the pigs?

   _____

3. What did Joe do after he watered the garden?

   _____

4. What did Joe do before he went swimming?

   _____

5. What did Joe do before he fed the pigs?

   _____

6. What did Joe do after he brushed the horses?

   _____

B. Answer the questions.
Use the picture on page 28.

1. Did Joe brush the horses before or after he fed the pigs?

   He brushed the horses after he fed the pigs.

2. Did Joe pick apples before or after he went swimming?

   _____

3. Did Joe milk the cows before or after he gathered the eggs?

   _____

4. Did Joe eat lunch before or after he watered the garden?

   _____

4. Did Joe pick apples before or after he ate lunch?

   _____

C. Number the pictures.
Read the sentences. Number the boxes in the correct order.

Jenny went to sleep after she took a bath.
She did her homework after she ate dinner.
She watched TV before she took a bath.
She did her homework before she watched TV.

Let's Learn

A. Match to make sentences.
Then match each sentence with the correct picture.

1. Julie forgot to tighten the saddle,

   a. so the cat got out.

2. The plants died

   b. so she fell off the horse.

3. Bill forgot to shut the door,

   c. so he got a sunburn.

4. Brad forgot to wear a hat,

   d. because Meg forgot to water them.

B. Make sentences.
Write sentences with the same meaning. Use "because" or "so."

1. The farmer forgot to close the gate, so the sheep got out.

<u>The sheep got out because the farmer</u>
<u>forgot to close the gate.</u>

2. Alison woke up late because she forgot to set the alarm clock.

<u>Alison forgot</u>
_____

3. Susan got wet because she forgot to bring an umbrella.

<u>Susan</u>
_____

4. Tom ate too much candy, so he got a stomachache.

<u>Tom</u>
_____

C. Complete the sentences. Use "because" or "so."

1. Willie got a sunburn _____ he forgot to wear a hat.

2. Brian forgot to close the door, _____ the dog got out.

3. Lidia forgot to water the garden, _____ the plants died.

4. Evan fell off the horse _____ he forgot to tighten the saddle.

D. Complete the sentences.

1. What happened?

   She forgot to bring an umbrella, _____

   _____

2. What happened?

   They woke up late _____

   _____

3. What happened?

   The farmer forgot to close the gate, _____

   _____

4. What happened?

   The flowers died _____

   _____

Let's Read

A. Fill in the blanks. Complete the crossword.

| farmers' market |
| quilts |
| produce |
| square dancing |
| baked goods |
| fresh |

Last Friday Mr. Miller's class visited a _____ in Somerville.
(1)

They learned about the market and tasted some delicious food.

The Somerville Farmers' Market is 50 years old. It started in a small barn.

Every Saturday farmers from the community came and sold _____
(2)

_____ from their farms.
(3)

Now the market is bigger. Besides produce, farmers also sell crafts, like

handmade _____, and _____, like bread
(4)   (5)

and pies. On Saturday night there is music and _____.
(6)

B. Find the words.
Read the story above and circle these words.

1. community

2. handmade

3. crafts

4. barn

C. Unscramble the questions. Write the answers.

visited	farmers'	a
market	who	?

1. _____

_____

farmers	sell	?
	what	did

2. _____

_____

what	Saturday	is	?
there	night	on	

3. _____

_____

D. Match and connect.

1. produce •   • not frozen

2. baked goods •   • fruits and vegetables

3. fresh •   • made by hand

4. handmade •   • baked food, like bread and pies

E. Fill in the blanks.
Use the letters "l" or "r." Then draw pictures.

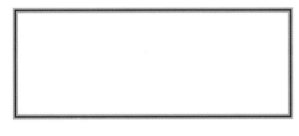

1. My ca___t can't sta___t because there's sa___t on this pa___t.

2. The man in the ki___t is in a ca___t on a qui___t.

Fill in the blanks.

1. Shirley Smith got up in the dark _____ the sun was up.

   _____ she drank her coffee, she _____ her coffee

   cup. Shirley Smith _____ _____ her pants. Shirley

   Smith _____ the plants. Shirley Smith _____ to town

   _____ the sun was up.

2. Peter Potts got out of bed _____ the sun was up.

   _____ he made his coffee, he _____ his coffee cup.

   Peter Potts _____ his pants. Peter Potts _____ on

   his plants. Peter Potts _____ _____ to bed

   _____ the sun was up.

A. Complete the list.

Read the sentences. Then write the farmer's activities in the right order.

Farmer Johnson fed the pigs before he watered the garden.

He milked the cows after he gathered the eggs.

He fed the pigs after he brushed the horses.

He gathered the eggs after he ate breakfast.

He milked the cows before he brushed the horses.

1. First he ate breakfast. _____

2. Then _____

3. _____

4. _____

5. _____

6. _____

B. Write the questions.

1. Gary   Why did Gary get wet? _____

   Because he forgot to bring an umbrella.

2. Josh   _____

   Because he forgot to wear a hat.

3. Kate   _____

   Because she forgot to tighten the saddle.

C. Make sentences.

Look at Exercise B above. Tell what happened to Gary, Josh, and Kate. Use "so."

1. Gary _____

2. Josh _____

3. Kate _____

Let's Review

A. Fill in the blanks. Complete the crossword.

Jim: The show is going to start soon.

Are you _____ (1) ?

Beth: _____ (2) .

Jim: You _____ (3) great!

Beth: Thanks. So do you.

Brian: Those apple chips look _____ (4) .

Bob: Actually, I'm kind of _____ (5) of apple chips.

Brian: I'll _____ (6) lunches with you.

Bob: It's a _____ (7) !

B. Write the questions.

1. **Whose cap is this?**
   It's his.

2. _____
   They're hers.

3. _____
   It's mine.

4. _____
   It's hers.

5. _____
   They're mine.

6. _____
   They're his.

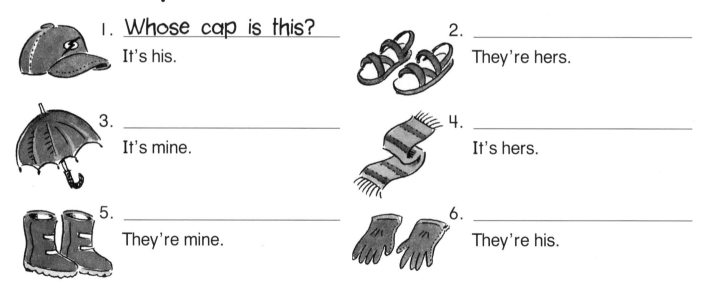

C. What about you?

What do you do before you go to school? What do you do after you come home?

_____

_____

D. Complete the sentences.

Use "because" or "so."

1. Anton got wet _____

_____

2. Bonnie forgot to tighten the saddle, _____

_____

3. Brenda forgot to wear a hat, _____

_____

4. _____ Tony forgot to

close the door.

E. Answer the questions.

1. Which boy is David?

<u>David is the boy who</u>
<u>is playing a computer game.</u>

2. Which boy is Max?

_____

_____

3.  Which girl is Karen?

_____

_____

4. Which girl is Sara?

_____

_____

A. Write the words. Complete the crossword.

1. _____

2. _____

3. _____

4. _____

5. _____

6. _____

7. _____

8. _____

9. _____

B. Unscramble, write, and draw.

Here are three presents. What are they?

1. d e y t d
   r b a e

   _____

2. y k e
   n h i a c

   _____

3. x b o f o
   e o o c c a h l t s

   _____

C. Answer the questions.

Jackie is buying presents for her family. What should she buy?

1. Jackie's grandmother likes chocolates and candy.
   What should Jackie buy for her grandmother?

   _____

2. Jackie's baby sister likes toys and dolls.
   What should Jackie buy for her baby sister?

   _____

3. Jackie's father likes to cook.
   What should Jackie buy for her father?

   _____

4. Jackie's grandfather likes clothes.
   What should Jackie buy for her grandfather?

   _____

5. Jackie's mother has a lot of keys.
   What should Jackie buy for her mother?

   _____

Let's Learn

A. Fill in the blanks. Use "should" or "shouldn't."

Joey is going to an expensive restaurant for the first time.
What should he do? What shouldn't he do?

1. He _____ blow bubbles in his milk.

2. _____ talk with his mouth full.

3. _____ run around.

4. _____ sit up straight.

5. _____ use his napkin.

Write two more sentences about Joey.

6. He should _____

7. He shouldn't _____

B. How should you act in a library?

Use the words in the box to make two lists.

	You should...	You shouldn't...
be quiet	_____	_____
sing		
run	_____	_____
sleep		
study	_____	_____
walk		

Now think of two more things for each list.

_____ _____

_____ _____

C. Make sentences. Use "should" or "shouldn't."

1. take an umbrella

   He _____

2. wear boots

   _____

3. wear a coat

   _____

4. wear a cap

   _____

D. Answer the questions.

1. Should she wash the dishes? _____

2. Should she feed the dog? _____

3. Should she watch TV? _____

4. Should she do her homework? _____

5. Should she read a comic book? _____

A. Choose the correct words to fill in the blanks.

Dear Ally,

Yesterday I got _____ again. I was late for school
(organized / in trouble)

_____ I _____ find my book bag. I had
(because / so)   (can't / couldn't)

to _____ and do my homework
(stay outside / stay after school)

_____. I was _____ because I
(over again / under again)   (happy / upset)

_____ soccer practice. What should I do?
(have / missed)

Yours truly,

Bill

Dear Bill,

The _____ to your _____ is easy. You should
(question / answer)   (problem / answer)

get _____. You should find a _____ place
(in trouble / organized)   (special / small)

for your book bag. Your things will be _____ to find. You _____
(easy / hard)   (will / won't)

be late and you won't _____ soccer practice _____.
(have / miss)   (anymore / anywhere)

Yours truly,

Ally

B. Read the letters. Write the names.

Read each letter to Ally. Write the name from each letter on the matching answer from Ally.

Dear Ally,
Yesterday I got in trouble again. I fell asleep in class because I was tired. What should I do?
Yours truly,
Sara

Dear Ally,
My things are always hard to find. What should I do?
Yours truly,
Mark

Dear Ally,
Yesterday I got in trouble again. I was late for school because I woke up late. What should I do?
Yours truly,
Steve

Dear _____,

You should get organized. You should clean your room and find a special place for your things.

Yours truly,

Ally

Dear _____,

You should go to bed earlier. Then you won't be tired anymore.

Yours truly,

Ally

Dear _____,

You should use an alarm clock. Then you won't wake up late anymore.

Yours truly,

Ally

C. Fill in the blanks. Complete the crossword.

1. Herbie _____ the
   (1)

   _____ _____
   (2)   (3)

   say a _____.
         (4)

2. The _____ man in the
        (5)

   _____ is _____
   (6)   (7)

   a _____ _____.
     (8)   (9)

Fill in the blanks.

Should I take my

 _____?

Do you think it's going to

_____?

Should I _____ my

_____ today?

I think you _____.

You should _____

your _____.

I _____ it's going

to _____ today.

Should I wear my

_____?

Do you think it's going to

_____?

Should I _____ my

_____ today?

I _____.

You should _____

your _____.

I _____ it's going

to _____ today.

Write the questions and answers.

Use the words in the box to answer the questions.

scarf	watch
soccer ball	book
cookbook	yo-yo

1. Danny's grandmother likes to cook.

   What should Danny buy for his grandmother?

   He should buy her a _____

2. Danny's father collects watches.

   _____

   _____

3. Danny's little brother likes toys.

   _____

   _____

4. Danny's mother likes to read.

   _____

   _____

5. Danny's big sister likes clothes.

   _____

   _____

6. Danny's cousin likes to play soccer.

   _____

   _____

Let's Talk

A. Make a conversation.
Put the lines in the correct order.

Mike: Are you serious?

Jane: I'd go to the moon.

Jane: No, I'm just kidding.

Mike: If you could go anywhere, where would you go?

1. _____

2. _____

3. _____

4. _____

B. Match and connect.

1. If you could go anywhere, •   • who would you meet?

2. If you could do anything, •   • where would you go?

3. If you could buy anything, •   • what would you do?

4. If you could meet anyone, •   • what would you buy?

C. What about you?
Complete the sentences.

1. If I could go anywhere, I would _____

_____

2. If I could do anything, _____

_____

3. If I could buy anything, _____

_____

4. If I could meet anyone, _____

_____

D. Look at the pictures. Complete the sentences.

a pony	London	a motorbike	Honolulu	Mexico City	a TV star
go skydiving	go surfing	a CD player	a famous singer	go kayaking	a sports star

Robbie   Jill   Sandy

1. If Robbie could go anywhere, **he would go to** _____

   If Jill could go anywhere, _____

   If Sandy could go anywhere, _____

2. If Robbie could buy anything, _____

   If Jill _____

   If Sandy _____

3. If Robbie could meet anyone, _____

   If Jill _____

   If Sandy _____

4. If Robbie could do anything, _____

   If Jill _____

   If Sandy _____

A. Look at the map. Make sentences.

Mary would love to visit Europe. What could she do there?

1. Spain

   She could go to Spain and go to the art
   museums.

2. France

   _____

   _____

3. Greece

   _____

   _____

4. Austria

   _____

   _____

5. Italy

   _____

   _____

B. Connect and write.

What are they studying? Where could they go?

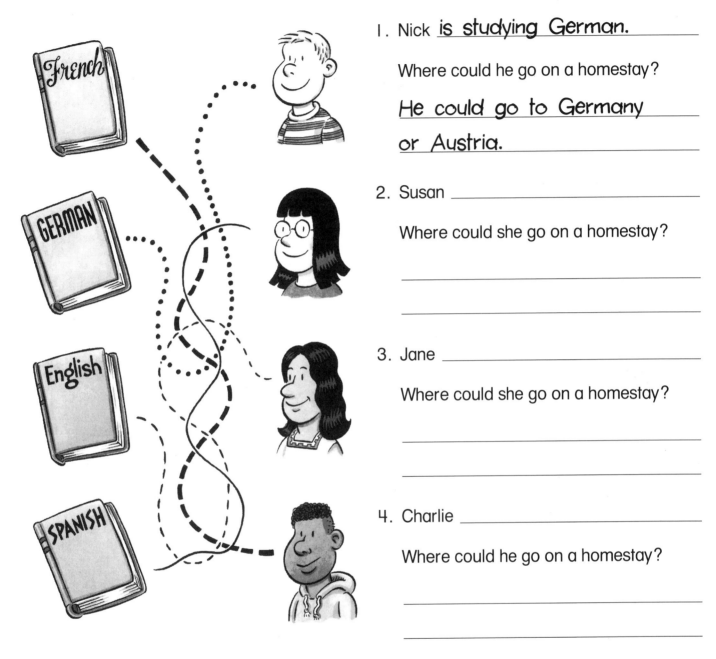

1. Nick <u>is studying German.</u>

   Where could he go on a homestay?

   <u>He could go to Germany</u>

   <u>or Austria.</u>

2. Susan _____

   Where could she go on a homestay?

   _____

   _____

3. Jane _____

   Where could she go on a homestay?

   _____

   _____

4. Charlie _____

   Where could he go on a homestay?

   _____

   _____

Let's Read

A. Answer the questions.

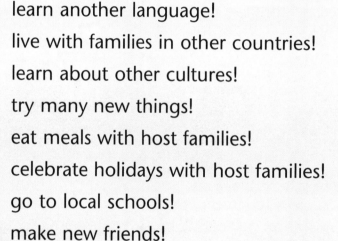

ABC FOREIGN STUDY

Director: Ann West

Why should you go on a homestay?
Because you can...

learn another language!

live with families in other countries!

learn about other cultures!

try many new things!

eat meals with host families!

celebrate holidays with host families!

go to local schools!

make new friends!

speak another language all day long!

1. Who is the director of ABC Foreign Study?

_____

2. Can you learn another language on a homestay?

_____

3. Who do you live with on a homestay?

_____

4. What can you do with your host family?

_____

B. Complete the following sentences.

1. Students on homestays live with _____ _____.

2. They eat _____ and _____ holidays with their

host families.

3. They go to _____ schools and make _____

_____.

4. They speak _____ language _____ day

_____.

C. What about you?

1. If you could go on a homestay, where would you go? _____

_____

2. Why? _____

_____

D. Find and circle the words.

| hands |
| pants |
| ant |
| painting |
| bend |
| ground |
| around |

k	p	f	l	x	v	q	e	y	b	t
k	s	a	r	v	a	q	m	y	e	j
k	p	f	i	x	a	r	m	a	n	t
h	p	p	a	n	t	s	o	y	d	b
a	s	k	c	v	t	s	m	u	r	t
n	p	q	l	x	r	i	q	y	n	g
d	m	f	g	r	o	u	n	d	r	d
s	p	f	l	x	v	q	m	g	r	t

Complete the questionnaire.

Answer the questions. Then ask a friend and your teacher.

	Your Friend	Your Teacher
1. If you could go anywhere, where would you go? _____ _____	_____ _____ _____	_____ _____ _____
2. If you could buy anything, what would you buy? _____ _____	_____ _____ _____	_____ _____ _____
3. If you could eat anything, what would you eat? _____ _____	_____ _____ _____	_____ _____ _____
4. If you could be anything, what would you be? _____ _____	_____ _____ _____	_____ _____ _____
5. If you could do anything, what would you do? _____ _____	_____ _____ _____	_____ _____ _____
6. If you could meet anybody, who would you meet? _____ _____	_____ _____ _____	_____ _____ _____

A. Complete the sentences. Connect.

| do anything | meet anyone | go anywhere | buy anything |

1. If he could _____ ,

   he'd go to Paris.

2. _____ ,

   he'd learn how to waterski.

3. _____ ,

   he'd buy a boat.

4. _____ ,

   he'd meet a soccer star.

B. Complete the sentences.

Count the letters and fill in the blanks. Use each word only once.

Austria
Australia
France
Mexico
German
English
French
Spanish

1. Pam is studying ___ ___ ___ ___ ___ ___ ___ .

   She could go to ___ ___ ___ ___ ___ ___ ___ ___ ___ .

2. Paul is studying ___ ___ ___ ___ ___ ___ .

   He could go to ___ ___ ___ ___ ___ ___ ___ .

3. Bill is studying ___ ___ ___ ___ ___ ___ .

   He could go to ___ ___ ___ ___ ___ ___ .

4. Mary is studying ___ ___ ___ ___ ___ ___ ___ .

   She could go to ___ ___ ___ ___ ___ ___ .

Let's Review

A. Match and connect.

Hey, Brian. What are you doing here?   I'd go to Australia.

Do you want some help?   Yes. I think it would be fun.

If you could go anywhere, where would you go?   I'm looking for a birthday present for my brother.

Are you serious?   OK. Thanks.

B. Complete the questions.

1. If you could do anything , what would you do?

   I'd go skydiving.

2. _____, who would you meet?

   I'd meet a famous TV star.

3. _____, what would you eat?

   I'd eat strawberry ice cream.

4. _____, where would you go?

   I'd go to France.

5. _____, what would you buy?

   I'd buy a new bicycle.

C. Write the answers.

1. Marty is studying French. Where could he go on a homestay?

   <u>He could go to Canada or France.</u>

2. Kelly is studying English. Where could she go on a homestay?

   _____

3. Gary is studying Spanish. Where could he go on a homestay?

   _____

4. Sally is studying German. Where could she go on a homestay?

   _____

D. Match and connect.

1. Bob's room is very messy. •   • He should study English.

2. James always wakes up very late. •   • He should clean his room.

3. Lee wants to go on a homestay
   to the United States. •   • He should take an umbrella.

4. Mick is going to school. It is
   going to rain today. •   • He should use an alarm clock.

Let's Talk

A. Make two sentences for each picture.

1. bored / boring

   The boy is <u>bored</u>.

   The book is _____.

2. scared / scary

   The monster is _____.

   The girl is _____.

3. tired / tiring

   Digging a hole is _____.

   The men are _____.

4. excited / exciting

   Tom is _____.

   Hang gliding is _____.

B. Answer the questions.

1. What did he say about the movie?

   _____

2. What did she say about the video?

   _____

3. What did he say about the comic book?

   _____

4. What did he say about the book?

   _____

C. Complete the sentences.

riding a roller coaster	sleeping in the dark
doing the laundry	splitting wood

1. Jamie is scared.

   He thinks _____ is scary.

2. Judy is excited.

   _____

3. Kevin and Jake are tired.

   _____

4. Lucy is bored.

   _____

D. What about you?
Write sentences about the videos.

exciting	funny	scary	boring

1. I think it looks _____
   _____

2. _____
   _____

3. _____
   _____

4. _____
   _____

A. Fill in the blanks.

1. slow → _____

2. _____ → carelessly

3. _____ → quickly

4. _____ → terribly

5. careful → _____

6. quiet → _____

7. _____ → beautifully

8. neat → _____

9. loud → _____

10. _____ → recklessly

B. Make sentences.

For each sentence, use one word from each box.

drove	played	cried
ran	sang	walked

quickly	carefully	recklessly
loudly	beautifully	terribly

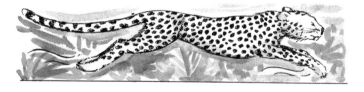

1. _____

2. _____

3. _____

4. _____

5. _____

6. _____

C. Make sentences.

Write two sentences for each picture. Use each word only once.

carelessly	neatly	slowly	loudly
carefully	quickly	recklessly	quietly

1. How should he walk?

   He should walk slowly.

   He shouldn't _____

2. How should they talk?

   _____

   _____

3. How should he write?

   _____

   _____

4. How should she ride?

   _____

   _____

D. What about you?

1. Do you usually talk quietly or loudly?

   _____

2. Do you usually walk quickly or slowly?

   _____

3. Do you usually draw beautifully or terribly?

   _____

4. Do you usually do your homework neatly or carelessly?

   _____

A. Find and circle the words.

camera
animation
projector
film
drawings
cartoon

c	i	n	t	f	l	u	y	l	a	c
j	u	b	l	w	c	a	m	e	r	a
e	r	s	p	o	e	n	s	q	n	r
h	v	e	a	k	f	i	l	m	i	t
t	z	a	f	t	e	m	m	t	u	o
o	d	d	r	a	l	a	y	z	g	o
p	r	o	j	e	c	t	o	r	a	n
s	a	r	s	l	e	i	m	y	k	r
i	w	t	e	g	h	o	r	n	i	u
l	i	n	s	t	b	n	p	a	s	n
l	n	w	e	n	i	p	d	l	a	t
i	g	q	u	n	o	r	h	t	e	y
c	s	a	c	a	r	r	s	i	t	j

B. Fill in the blanks.
Use the words above. Use every word.

Robert Smith's hobby is cartoon _____. Robert told his class how he

makes a _____. First he makes a lot of _____.

Then he uses a movie _____ to take a picture of each drawing. When the

_____ goes through a movie _____, we see all the

pictures one after the other. Robert says making a cartoon is a lot of work.

C. Put the sentences in the correct order.

_____ Robert shows the film through a movie projector.

_____ Robert makes the drawings.

_____ The pictures on the film go by quickly, so Pencil Man looks like he's moving.

_____ Robert takes a picture of each drawing.

D. Circle the correct word and fill in the blanks.

1.   winks
      wings

A bird has two _____.

2.   bank
      bang

Mr. Smith works in a _____.

3.   Ping
      pink

Mary's favorite color is _____.

4.   sing
      sink

There are dishes in the _____.

5.   Ping
      pink

The boys are playing _____-Pong.

6.   sing
      sink

Amy can _____ very well.

7.   wink
      wing

My mother is _____ing at me.

8.   bank
      bang

The door made a loud _____.

E. Read and draw.

Two small skunks played Ping-Pong in the sink.

Let's Chant

A. Fill in the blanks.

I couldn't _____ him. He spoke _____ quickly.

I _____
_____ him.
He _____
_____ fast.

I asked him to _____ it.
And he said it _____.
But I couldn't _____
him _____!

B. Match and connect the sentences.

1. We couldn't hear Mary because •

2. Jeff didn't win the race because •

3. The teacher couldn't read Pete's homework because •

4. We couldn't understand Tom because •

5. Jenny fell off her bicycle because •

• he wrote too carelessly.

• she sang too quietly.

• she rode too recklessly.

• he ran too slowly.

• he spoke too quickly.

A. Fill in the blanks.

tired	boring	exciting	scared	bored	excited	scary	tiring

1. John: This is fun! I love roller coasters!

   Sue: I don't like them. I think they're _____.

   John: No, they're not. They're _____.

   Sue: Well, I'm not _____. I'm _____.

2. Mary: This work is _____.

   Pete: I think so, too. I'm _____.

   Mary: Let's take a break.

   Pete: OK. Good idea!

3. Nick: What's the matter?

   Liz: I'm _____. I don't have anything to do.

   Nick: Why don't you watch TV?

   Liz: The TV programs are _____ today.

B. Answer the questions.

	slowly	quickly	carefully	recklessly	quietly	loudly
Dan rides a bike...		✓		✓		
Laura rides a bike...	✓		✓			
Dan speaks...	✓					✓
Laura speaks...		✓			✓	

1. How does Dan ride a bike?

   He rides quickly and recklessly.

2. How does Laura ride a bike?

   _____

3. How does Dan speak?

   _____

4. How does Laura speak?

   _____

— Let's Talk —

A. Match and connect.

1. We're moving! •   • I'll miss you, too.

2. When are you going? •   • I won't.

3. Do you want some help? •   • Oh, no! That's awful.

4. We'll miss you. •   • That would be great. Thanks.

5. Don't forget to write. •   • In two weeks.

B. Fill in the blanks.
Use the words in the box. You can use some words more than once.

| on | off | up | out |

1. pack _____

2. put _____

3. take _____

4. turn _____

5. mix _____

6. throw _____

7. turn _____

8. tear _____

C. Fill in the blanks.

1. take off   → took off _____

2. put on   → _____

3. tear up   → _____

4. pack up   → _____

5. throw out   → _____

6. turn on   → _____

7. mix up   → _____

8. turn off   → _____

D. Make three sentences for each picture.

1. He turned on the television.
   He turned the television on.
   He turned it on.

2. _____

   _____

   _____

3. _____

   _____

   _____

4. _____

   _____

E. Look at the pictures above and write questions.

1. _____

   Yes, she mixed them up.

2. _____

   Yes, he turned it on.

3. _____

   No, he didn't put them on.

4. _____

   Yes, he threw it out.

A. Match and connect.

1. Can you •   • in eighth grade?

2. Do you •   • ever seen a penguin?

3. Are you •   • ride a bicycle?

4. Did you •   • like to go swimming tomorrow?

5. Have you •   • like English?

6. Would you •   • go to school yesterday?

B. Fill in the blanks. Answer the questions.

Where	Which	What	Who
How	When	What time	

1. __What time__ do you usually get up?

_____

2. _____ is your birthday?

_____

3. _____ grade are you in?

_____

4. _____ long have you studied English?

_____

5. _____ is your best friend?

_____

6. _____ do you live?

_____

7. _____ do you like better, cake or ice cream?

_____

C. Fill in the blanks.

Read the answers and complete the questions.

1. _____ clean your room yet?  Yes. I did.

2. _____ play the piano?  No, but he can sing.

3. _____ ready?  No, I'm not. I have to put on my shoes.

4. _____ ever been to Paris?  No, but they have been to Spain.

5. _____ like to go shopping?  Yes, I'd love to.

6. _____ have any brothers or sisters?  Yes, she does. She has two brothers and one sister.

D. Make sentences.

1. I am _____

2. I can _____

3. I like to _____

4. I have to _____

───────── Let's Read ─────────

A. Fill in the blanks.

still
language
problem
study
long time

Benjamin: I have a _____.

Connie: What's the matter?

Benjamin: Every day I _____ hard, but I _____

can't speak English very well.

Connie: Don't worry. It takes a _____ _____

to learn a _____.

B. Complete the questions. Write the answers.

meaning	dictionary	improving	discouraged	look up

1. Do you think your English is _____?

   _____

2. Have you ever felt _____ about learning English?

   _____

3. Do you _____ every word in a _____,

   or do you try to guess the _____ from the story?

   _____

C. What about you?
What would you like to do to improve your English?

_____

_____

_____

_____

D. Fill in the questionnaire.

Answer the questions yourself. Then ask a friend.

	You	Your Friend
I. Have you ever watched a movie or TV show in English?		
2. Have you ever read a book or magazine in English?		
3. Do you ever listen to songs in English?		
4. Do you have a pen pal?		
5. Do you think English is easy?		
6. Do you like to speak English with other people?		

E. Unscramble the words and fill in the blanks.

1. The _____ with the _____
   b m a l   b o c m

   _____ on the _____.
   e j m u d p   t p s m u

2. The _____ had a _____
   r b u m l e p   p m b u

   on his _____.
   b h m t u

A. Match and connect.

1. When are you leaving? •

2. Where are you going? •

3. Don't forget to write. •

4. Good-bye, girls. •

• Good-bye, boys.

• We'll write to you tonight.

• We're leaving at six.

• We're going to France.

B. Write the questions and answers.

ROY

1. Where is Roy going? _____

_____

2. When is he leaving? _____

_____

LINDA

3. _____

_____

4. _____

_____

JEFF

5. _____

_____

6. _____

_____

Let's Listen

A. Change the sentences.

1. He packed up the toys.

   He packed them up.

2. She turned off the TV.

   _____

3. She turned on the light.

   _____

4. He put on his coat.

   _____

5. He threw out his old books.

   _____

6. She tore up the newspaper.

   _____

B. Unscramble the answers. Match and connect.

1. If you could meet anyone, who would you meet? •

   • | six   for   years   I've   English   studied |

   _____

2. How does it taste? •

   • | blue   I   one   the   like |

   _____

3. What do you have to do? •

   • | room   clean   have   to   I   my |

   _____

4. Which one do you like? •

   • | sour   It   tastes |

   _____

5. How long have you studied English? •

   • | star   a   movie   meet   I'd |

   _____

6. Where could you go on a homestay? •

   • | or   to   could   France   I   Canada   go |

   _____

A. Find and correct the mistakes.

English homework   Alex Brown   Class 6B

1. Tom said the movie was ~~excited~~. *exciting*
2. Yesterday I went to bed early because I was tiring.
3. I think sleeping in the dark is scary.
4. My father said splitting wood was tired.
5. I think doing the laundry is bored.

B. Unscramble the words. Answer the questions.

1. How should she talk?

u l d o y l

She should talk _____

2. How should they run?

u i k q c l y

_____

3. How should he walk?

l f c u a e r y l

_____

4. How should they write?

a y n l e t

_____

C. Write the answers.

1.  Did he mix up the cards?

_____

2.  Did she throw out the trash?

_____

3.  Did she turn off the TV?

_____

4.  Did he put on his sweater?

_____

D. Make your own questions. Write the answers.

1. What _____

_____

2. When _____

_____

3. Where _____

_____

4. Who _____

_____

5. Why _____

_____

6. Which _____

_____

7. How _____

_____

Read the questions and write a report.
Draw a picture.

My Hobbies

What is your favorite hobby? How long have you had this hobby?
Why do you like it? What other hobbies do you have?

_____

_____

_____

_____

_____

_____

_____

Draw a picture of one of your hobbies.